Mother

AN *Angel* TO WATCH OVER ME

SALLY DEFORD

Cover image: *Walk to Remember* © Jean Monti, licensed by The Greenwich Workshop, Inc.
www.greenwichworkshop.com.
Cover and book design by Mark Sorenson, © 2009 by Covenant Communications, Inc.
Published by Covenant Communications, Inc., American Fork, Utah.

Text/Lyrics © Sally DeFord.
Copyright © 2009 by Covenant Communications, Inc.
Printed in China
First Printing: March 2009

16 15 14 13 12 11 10 09   10 9 8 7 6 5 4 3 2 1

ISBN-13 978-1-59811-780-6
ISBN-10 1-59811-780-7

AN *Angel*
TO WATCH OVER ME

SALLY DEFORD

She watched by my cradle
through long, sleepless nights,

Jean Monti

*S*he taught me to pray
as she knelt by my side,

She guarded my childhood,
and all through the years,

In the arms of my mother,
I came to believe
That God sent an angel
to watch over me.

She taught me the meaning
of courage and faith,

$\mathcal{S}$he taught me to live
with the Lord as my strength,

She taught me to follow
the pathway He marked,

$\mathcal{S}$he guided my steps
when the journey grew dark,

And I know there were dangers
that I could not see,
But God sent an angel
to watch over me.

$\mathcal{S}$he taught me to serve
with a spirit that sings,

She taught me to seek
after heavenly things,

And because of her love
and her kindness and care,
Because of the place
that I hold in her prayers,

And because of her goodness,
I still believe
That God sent an angel
to watch over me.

Art Credits

Angel